D0131121

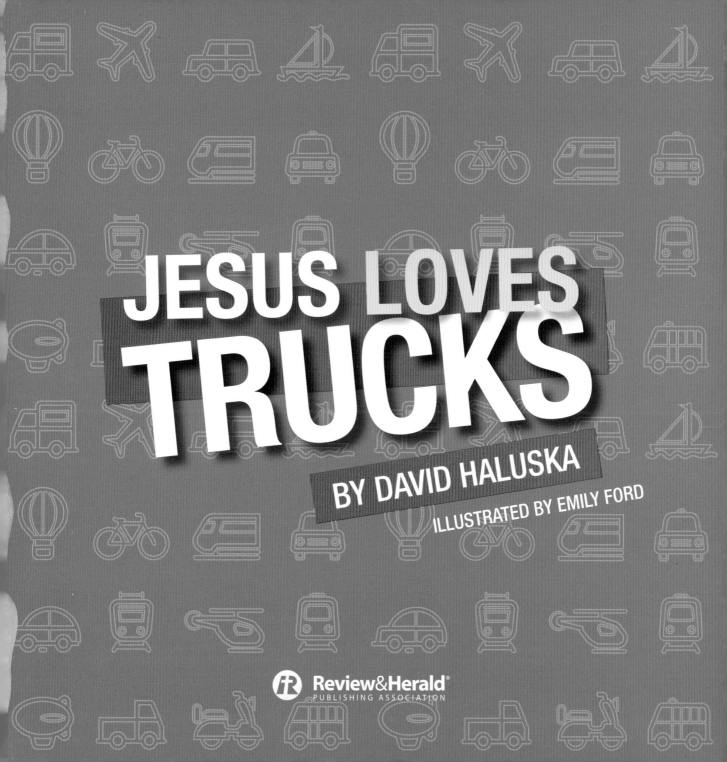

JESUS LOVES TRUCKS

BY DAVID HALUSKA

ILLUSTRATED BY EMILY FORD

Review & Herald®
PUBLISHING ASSOCIATION

Copyright © 2014 by North American Division Stewardship Ministries
Published by Review and Herald® Publishing Association, Hagerstown, MD 21741-1119

All rights reserved. No portion of this book may be reproduced, stored in a retrieval system, or transmitted in any form or by any means (electronic, mechanical, photocopy, recording, scanning, or other), except for brief quotations in critical reviews or articles, without the prior written permission of the publisher.

Review and Herald® titles may be purchased in bulk for educational, business, fund-raising, or sales promotional use. For information, e-mail SpecialMarkets@reviewandherald.com.

The Review and Herald® Publishing Association publishes biblically based materials for spiritual, physical, and mental growth and Christian discipleship.

This book was
Edited by JoAlyce Waugh
Copyedited by James Cavil
Designed by Emily Ford / Review and Herald® Design Center
Cover photo © Maranatha
Cover and interior illustration by Emily Ford / Review and Herald® Design Center
Typeset: 18/27 Helvetica Neue (TT) Bold

PRINTED IN U.S.A.

18 17 16 15 14   5 4 3 2 1

Library of Congress Cataloging-in-Publication Data

Haluska, David.
  Jesus loves trucks / David Haluska.
      pages cm
1. Missions--Juvenile literature. 2. Missionaries--Transportation--Juvenile literature. 3. Missionaries--Travel--Juvenile literature. I. Title.
  BV2065.H25 2013
  266'.6732--dc23

                          2012048368

ISBN 978-0-8280-2719-9

FOR MY SONS,
NATHAN AND JOSHUA,

JESUS LOVES TRUCKS.

Jesus Loves Trucks.

These trucks haul wood
and metal and bricks
so that people can build
a church.

Have you everseen a big truck?

JESUS LOVES AIRPLANES.

6

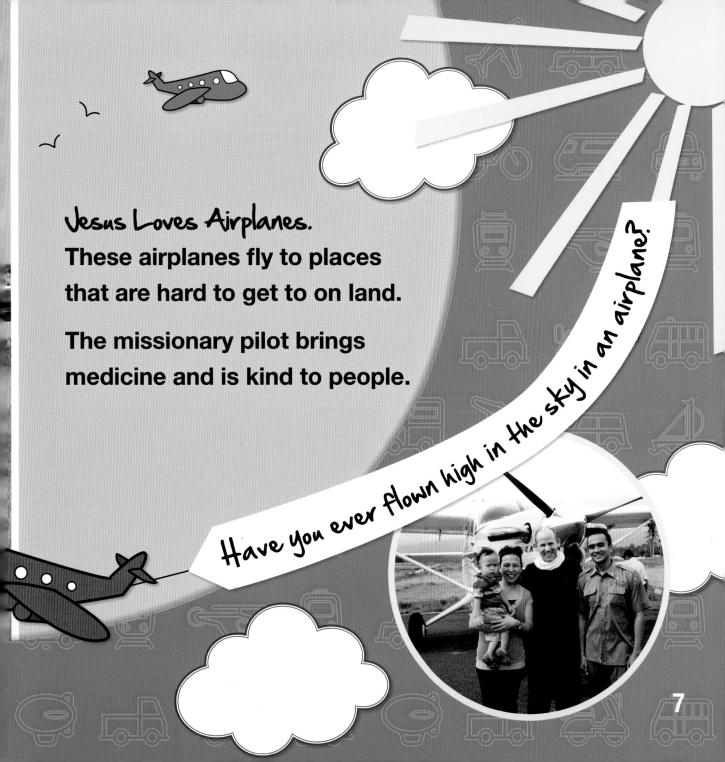

Jesus Loves Airplanes.
These airplanes fly to places
that are hard to get to on land.

The missionary pilot brings
medicine and is kind to people.

Have you ever flown high in the sky in an airplane?

7

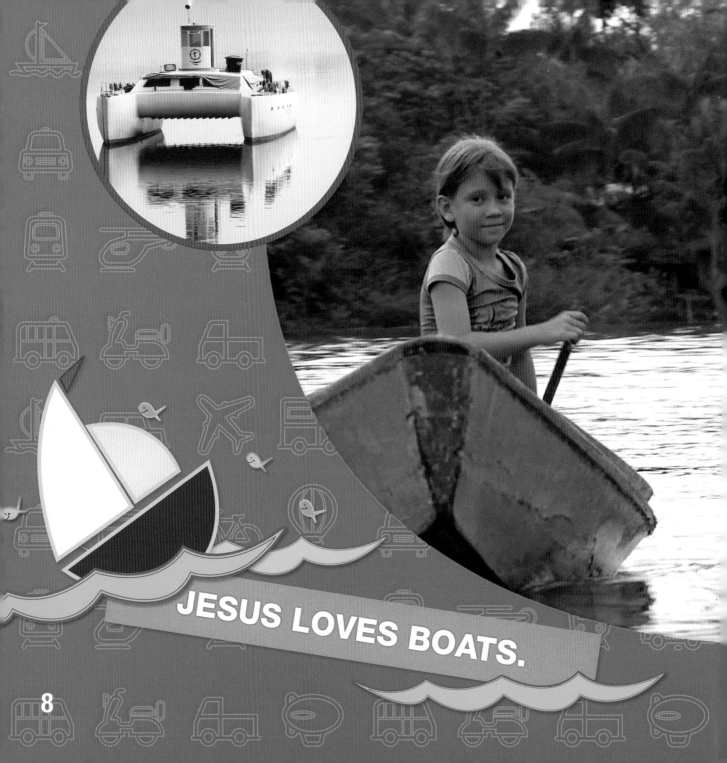

JESUS LOVES BOATS.

8

Jesus Loves Boats.

These boats float on rivers and oceans to take the story of Jesus to places where water is the only road.

Have you ever sailed on a boat?

JESUS LOVES CAMPERS.

10

Jesus Loves Campers.

This camper travels
to camp meeting.

It is a home for a family
to stay in during the
meetings.

Have you ever slept in a camper?

JESUS LOVES 4x4 VEHICLES.

Jesus Loves 4X4 Vehicles.

These 4x4s bounce through deep mud and holes in the roads.

They can go where cars can't go, and bring missionary doctors to sick people.

VROOM! VROOM!

Have you ever seen a 4x4 stuck in the mud?

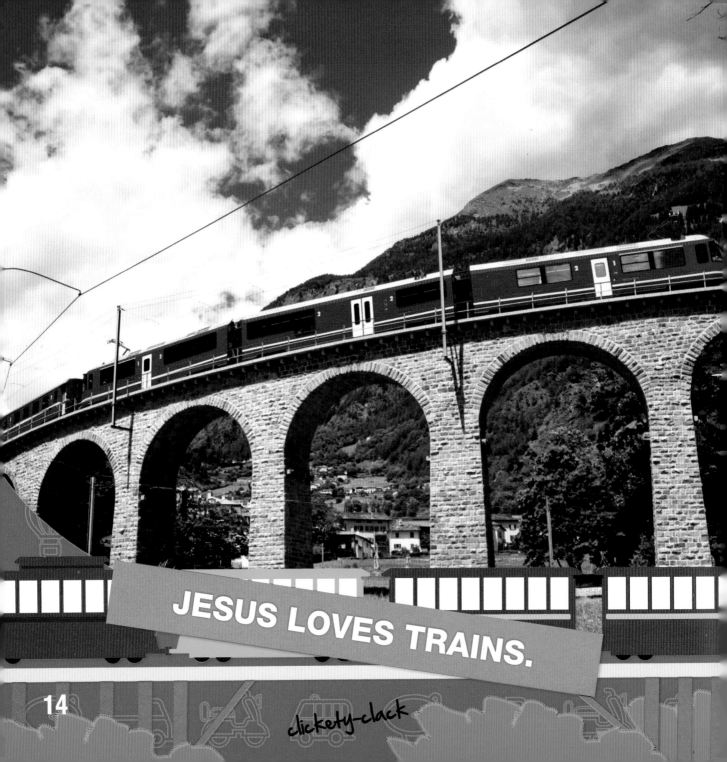

JESUS LOVES TRAINS.

clickety-clack

Jesus Loves Trains.

This train takes people to faraway places.

They will share the story of Jesus with the new friends they meet.

Have you ever heard a train's whistle?

clickety-clack

toot-toot!

clickety-clack

clickety-clack

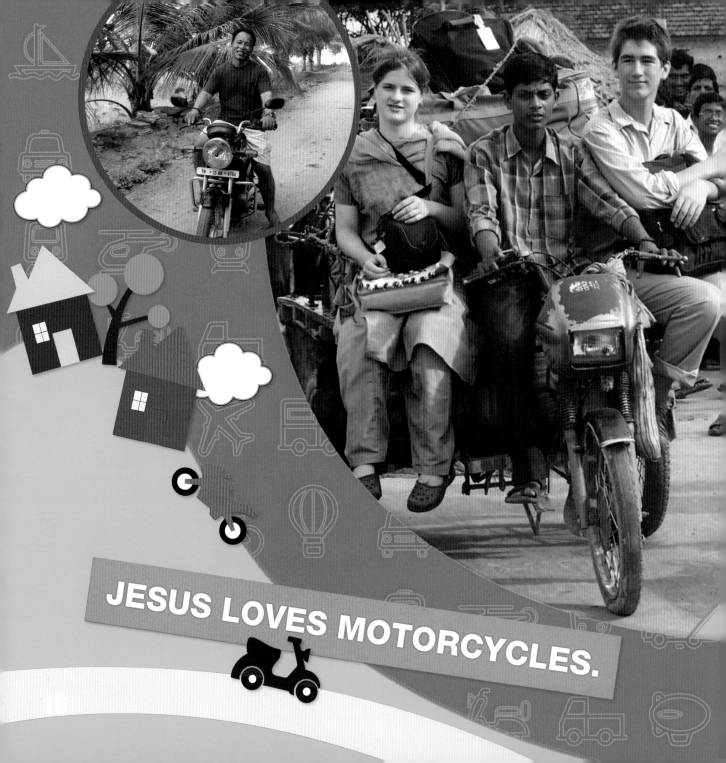

JESUS LOVES MOTORCYCLES.

Jesus Loves Motorcycles.
These motorcycles take
people from house to house.
The people share books that
tell about God.

Have you ever taken a ride on a motorcycle?

JESUS LOVES BUSES.

Jesus Loves Buses.

This bus can hold many people.

Some of the people are going to church to learn about God.

Have you ever been a passenger on a bus?

JESUS LOVES WELL DIGGERS.

Jesus Loves Well Diggers.

This well digger truck helps provide clean water to boys and girls in Africa, keeping their bodies healthy and happy for Jesus.

Have you ever dug a deep hole?

21

JESUS LOVE VANS.

Jesus Loves Vans.

These vans carry
happy people to many
neighborhoods.

They tell everyone that Jesus
loves them.

Have you ever taken a trip in a van?

EXIT 82

23

JESUS LOVES MOTOR RICKSHAWS.

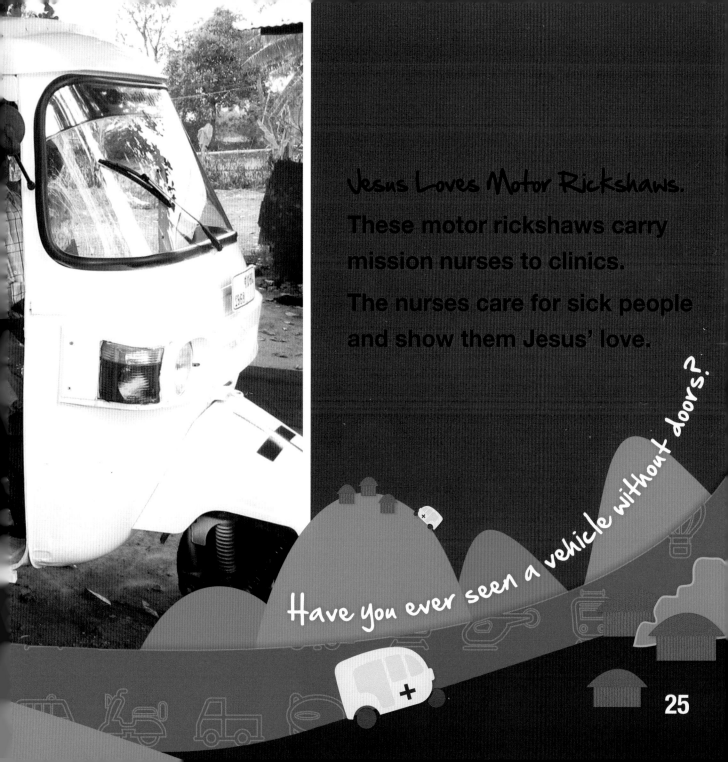

Jesus Loves Motor Rickshaws.

These motor rickshaws carry mission nurses to clinics.

The nurses care for sick people and show them Jesus' love.

Have you ever seen a vehicle without doors?

JESUS LOVE TRACTORS.

Jesus Loves Tractors.
These tractors work on a mission farm where the local people learn ways to grow their own food.

Have you ever been to a farm?

JESUS LOVES FIRE TRUCKS.

Jesus Loves Fire Trucks.

Missionaries help train firefighters.

This fire truck is stationed at an airport to keep travelers safe.

POHNPEI INTERNATIONAL AIRPORT C-4

FIRE HOUSE

NEE-NAA NEE-NAA

Have you ever heard a fire truck's siren?

What do you have that helps you share Jesus' love?

Can you set the table?

Can you share your trike?

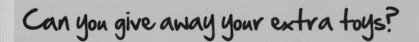

Can you keep someone dry?

Can you give away your extra toys?

JESUS LOVES YOU, TOO!

PICTURES PROVIDED BY:

Adventist Mission

http://www.adventistmission.org/
(pp. 7; 8, 9)

Victoria was 8 years old when she started a Bible study for children in her community. To learn more about her and other remarkable people who are working for Jesus, visit the Web site above.

Doctors Without Borders

http://www.doctorswithoutborders.org/slideshows
(pp. 12, 13; 24)

Ansley Howe has worked as a nurse with Doctors Without Borders for the past few years. To learn more about the places these doctors and nurses go, check out their Web site.

MAHI International

http://www.mahi-intl.org/MAHI_International/Home.html
(pp. 28, 29)

Jimmy Phillips was an MAHI International volunteer who came to Pohnpei, Micronesia, to document the team of health-care professionals who served in the various island communities. To learn more about MAHI International and the work they do, check out their Web site.

Maranatha

http://www.maranatha.org/Template_
Load.aspx?PageID=242

(pp. 4; 20, 21)

These trucks were used to build schools
and bring clean water to villages in Africa.
To Learn more about Maranatha and the
work they do, check out their Web site.

Outpost Centers International

http://www.outpostcenters.org/

(pp. 6; 8; 12; 16; 23; 24, 25; 26, 27)

To learn more about the mission
of Outpost Centers International and the
work they do, check out their Web site.

You Can Be a Missionary

http://www.adventist.org/service/missionaries/

(pp. 16, 17; 18, 19; 22)

Matthew White and his wife spent a year teaching in
South Korea. Ricky Barbosa went to India on a short-
term mission trip with his church. To learn more about
what it means to be a missionary, check out the Web site
above.

Unless otherwise noted, all photos are © Thinkstock.com.